Top 5 Fastest
Way
to
Make Money
Online

Get out of Debt
&
Be Financially Free

Malcolm Berry

Table of Contents

1. The Benefits of Making Money Online
2. Affiliate Marketing
3. Freelance Writing
4. Ebook Publishing
5. Domain Flipping
6. Google Adsense
7. How to Achieve Success

Introduction

What is the absolute fastest way to make money online? I'm a firm believer that making money online as quick as possible is the most important factor for your online success. If you want to make money online now, then you have to follow any strategy that has a proven track record of generating money as soon as possible. With the world being your marketplace you have many different options. The key is not to lose your focus which many people do and that stops them from earning money. For people who think they don't need no money to earn money online better get that out of their head. No matter what you do online, it takes money. Yes there are success stories that started with nothing, but those are rare. Anyone can tell people how to make money online, but the success will depend on many different factors. The key to online success is never give up and take all the advice that is given to you. You may not use it all, but it never hurts to listen to successful people. It's true, the fastest or quickest approach to making money can be short lived if you don't plan out your business. But, it's also very powerful approach when you can manage and accumulate the return for building your long term goal. In short, you can implement short term strategy to make money online but your vision of accumulating your money must always be long term.

Chapter I

The Benefits and Challenges of Making Money Online

The Internet has become a wealth of information to millions and at the same time a source of wealth for a lot of people. It has created a new industry that is generating lots of jobs and has become an opportunity for a lot of people profiting directly online.

These individuals have even left their day jobs to focus on working full time on the Internet when they realized that they have been earning more than they are used to. Moreover, they have discovered that the benefits of making money online definitely outweigh the risks involved.

If you are still testing the waters, here are some advantages that might help convince you to take the plunge:

You can earn the same or even bigger income

Many people started with the idea that working online will be another way to augment their own income, with the primary source of funds being their real job. However, later, they found out that their additional income has been surpassing their normal salaries, and for less time as well.

This is usually the time that they decide to quit their former jobs and become online professionals. Most of them have become online writers, programmers, designers, and marketers, to name a few.

Working online has given them the financial freedom that they could not be able to attain if they were working for a brick-and-mortar company.

You can work at home, or everywhere if you want to

Working online simply requires you a personal computer or a laptop and a working Internet connection. For those with families, this means more time with their spouse and children.

It also reduces expenses. Incidentally, this becomes one reason why you earn more; you have lesser overhead expenses.

You can reduce stress

A lot of people who have experienced stress often get them while still working in the office. Sources of stress can be the amount of work, deadlines, and the pressures you get from co-workers and especially from your boss.

Working online still has deadlines, but you personally can set time, and you can choose how much work you want to accomplish. This means you can work better. You have the freedom to choose the environment where you want to work. You make all the decisions, making you your own boss.

You can live your life the way you want it

You are not bound by time and you are free to decide what is best for you. Like all things, you will have to work for it.

But when you have your stride, you will notice that you now have more time to do things. In fact, even more opportunities will open up for you. Instead of being tied up to a desk, you can now have a chance of having a better quality of life.

Commute

People living in cities with heavy traffic spend hours in the traffic, wasting great deal of their time. This time could have been used to do something productive if they were at home making money online. Those who work online do not have to worry about commuting on a daily basis.

Boss

This is one of the main reasons why people often give up on the traditional ways of working and prefer working at home. There has been a bad history of people leaving their jobs because their boss is not fair and working under him simply depresses them.

When you are making money online, you do not have to worry about pleasing your boss or controlling your anger because of an unimportant matter.

Passion

Making money online by doing something you are passionate about is always a great feeling. These people do not really worry about the money, but for them, the passion matters the most. For example, those who have a flair for writing can work online and work towards their passion.

An increasing number of people are appreciating the immense opportunities of making money online. In fact, a significant number of people have had great success in earning money online and do not regret the decision they made.

In this light, it is worth exploring such opportunities in order to make an informed decision. Most importantly, learning how to effectively penetrate this niche is a matter of paramount importance.

Quite a number of online money making opportunities require zero capital. However, you may still need some money. For example, even if you are working from home, it is important that you set up a home office.

Have a Disciplined in Schedule

Earning money online is not a gateway to resting all the time. On the contrary, it requires that you exercise a lot of discipline in your schedule.

It is not uncommon to find that personal chores overlap with office hours. If you have a family and children, let the children know that you need to concentrate during work. Similarly, do not allow friends to pop in to your house as they wish.

Challenges

One of the greatest challenges facing online opportunities is the possibility of being scammed. In order to avoid this, carry out a thorough research of the company in question. Second, working online could translate into more working hours. Set aside a certain hours that you do not work. This is your personal time for relaxation and recreation.

The value of making money online cannot be underestimated. In this regard, you ought to look for a reputable source of information on how to make money online.

We have accumulated vast experience on the most effective and sustainable way of making money online. We are going to help you in introducing you to the basics and take you through every step of the way to your success.

You can clearly see how the internet has become a great medium to make money these days. It has provided opportunities to people to earn money in any field, and many people benefit from it as well.

In the next chapters, I will discuss the top five fastest ways to start making money online. I hope you will start taking action after reading these chapters.

Chapter II
Affiliate Marketing

There is no doubt that everyone wants to make more money. If they are able to earn money online especially from home, then it becomes their dream job.

Due to current economic situation in the world, more people have been focusing on online jobs hoping to make few dollars to thousands of dollars monthly by doing various tasks on the internet.

Affiliate marketing started out as a promotion strategy, where people were paid to refer a business to potential customers. However, today it has emerged as one of the most fastest and recommended methods to earn some extra cash online.

This short chapter on how to make money online with affiliate marketing discusses the foundation of this venture.

Probably you would already be having a bit of an idea what affiliate marketing entails, if you are familiar with the world affiliate. In affiliate marketing, you promote othere peoples product or service in exchange for set percentage of commission or fee.

For example, if you find a product online which is very helpful to you and you feel that it can help others too if you can refer the product to them; you can get an affiliate link of that product from its seller and start to promote it.

This way, if anyone buys that product using your affiliate, you will receive affiliate commission or fee. It can be paralleled to the job of a real estate agent or a real-life car salesman in which salesman make a commission on the final sale price of a commodity.
There are various pros and cons related to affiliate marketing which should be kept in mind before indulging into it.

Pros:

First, you are helping both buyer and seller while making money for yourself because you are referring valuable products to a buyer and helping sellers by increasing his sales.

Second, the best thing about affiliate marketing is, you do not have to deal with product shipment hassle, quality control myths and customer support issue. You are just refering the product of a seller and earning your commission if a visitor makes a purchase.

Stick to a few good products

It is tempting to spread yourself across a range of products; after all, you could set up multiple streams of income. This is a mistake most newbies make. Handling too many products can get overwhelming. With a handful of main products, you can focus better on promoting it aggressively.

Choose products relevant to your website, preferably those you have used. Also consider the market demand and the affiliate payout for the products you intend to promote on your site.

Work to build a content-rich site

What idea would you get from a site that has nothing but few images and affiliate links thrown together? You definitely wouldn't want to buy from them because the commission motive is quite clear.

Create a website such that it builds credibility in the minds of website visitors. Your promotion of the affiliate product should be subtle. Write informative blogs related to your niche. How-to-guides and product reviews tend to be very helpful. Whatever content you post to your site, it should have an authorial tone to it.

No promotion, no money

There is simply no substitute for promotion. Where and how you promote the products will determine how many clicks or views you get. The affiliate links should be placed in strategic places, where they get maximum exposure.

These include the header bar and at the top or bottom of a post. Links can also be embedded in the post. As part of promotion, you can also sync your website with social media profiles.

Your social connections will be notified about new products and updates. It also brings in a lot of targeted traffic. You can submit articles to article directories with an affiliate link included to get click through traffic.

The right merchant

This is another tip many affiliate marketers overlook when considering how to make money online with affiliate marketing.
The fact that you are promoting a product or service on your website means you endorse them.

First, choose a product and merchant you are comfortable promoting. The merchant should be trustworthy and reliable. They should prize quality and offer good customer service. Do a bit of research before you settle down for a merchant.

Track your affiliate setup

At the end of every month, you should review the performance of your affiliate setup. What is the conversion rate? Is your investment of time and effort worth the profit you earn? Are there enough conversions? You can tweak a few strategies to increase the conversions.

Build an email list

It is one thing to have one-time visitors and quite another to have those who keep coming back for more. By getting people to subscribe to your site, you can update them on the latest blog pots as well as product offers. Don't force them to sign up for newsletters or subscribe to your site.

Let it be a voluntary decision. You don't want to be a spammer.

Cons:

First, why people need to sell products via affiliate marketing? It can be one of those products which cannot be sold due to its low quality or over stated benefits. Therefore, if you will promote those types of products, you will be making people lose money for insignificant products.

Second, it is not easy to sell affiliate products since the original seller of that product needs assistance from affiliates to sell it. Therefore, you can be wasting your time and efforts on something just doesn't sell.

Therefore, it is highly recommended to promote or sell high quality products via affiliate marketing because this way you will not only earn money but will help others (both buyer and seller) by referring valuable and quality products.

Important Components Your Business Must Have

Making money online with affiliate marketing is possible if you are willing to commit the required time and effort into making it work. If you want to be successful in this business, you will want to observe the things that successful affiliate marketers have done so that you will be able to model after them.

There are 3 important components that your business must have if you want to earn long-term income.

1. Promoting Affiliate Product That is Proven to Sell
2. High Converting Squeeze Page to Collect Visitors' Details
3. Consistent flow of traffic to the squeeze page

Promoting Affiliate Product That Is Proven To Sell

You will want to make sure that you are promoting products that the customers are willing to purchase. It is not a wise decision to assume whether the product is sellable on the market.

You will want to ensure that you have done some research so that you will be able to understand the problems that your customers are facing and recommend them relevant products.

Successful affiliate marketers will be very picky of the product that they are promoting as they want to make sure that the product is good. The good thing is that there are many good affiliate networks around and you should not have any problem finding any good and relevant products to promote to your customers.

High Converting Squeeze Page To Collect Visitors' Details

If you want to make money online and earn long-term income, you must have your own list of subscribers. Successful affiliate marketers will always ensure that they have an opt in form on their website so that they can collect visitors' details. In order to achieve that goal, most of them use the squeeze page as their website.

The smart marketers will constantly tweak and edit their squeeze page so that they will be able to get the best conversion from the traffic that they are driving to the website.

It is important to make sure that the squeeze page is simple looking, have an attention grabbing headline and an obvious call to action message. All these different components will help to ensure that the squeeze page will be able to get the best conversions.

Consistent flow of traffic to the squeeze page

The core reason successful affiliate marketers are making money online consistently is because there are consistent stream of traffic going to their website.

When you are just starting, it is important that you focus the majority of your time on traffic generation activities that will help to get consistent flow of traffic back to your website.

There are free and paid methods of traffic generation method and you want to choose the method that suits your situation. It is advisable to stay focus on mastering one method at a time before proceeding to the next method.

Once you have mastered several methods, you will want to plan your own traffic plan so that you will know the actions that you have to take on a daily basis.

Essential Characteristics

Maybe you have heard all of the wonderful opportunities that an affiliate marketing business can give you. Surely it can't be as easy as some of those sales pages make it seem, or can it?
The answer is "yes" and "no." Yes, you can get to the place where you have

automated systems in place. Yes, you can get to the point to where you may only have to "work" a few hours per week.

Here are three essential characteristics that you need to make it in the affiliate marketing business:

1. You must be prepared to work. At first making money online with an affiliate marketing business sounds really glamorous. You are your own boss. You set your own schedule. You can go on vacation anytime you like.

The flipside to all that freedom is that you must be extremely disciplined. Otherwise, you will spend too much time not working. You won't make money, of course, if all you do is "vacation" all the time. Everyone knows that, but you do have to be prepared to work in order to succeed.

2. You must be patient. With a new venture, there is always a learning curve. There may be many of those curves. You

may or may not be familiar with computers. You probably will eventually want to at least learn some basic HTML code. That will take some time.

Most careers require a certain amount of hours of "schooling." Think of your learning curve as hours invested in schooling. Also much of what you do to make money online with affiliate marketing will have a cumulative effect.

Once a website is built, that work is done, but the benefit will remain. Once an article is accepted by an article directory, that work is done, but the article will be out there to be read for years to come. So, be prepared to work, and be patient. Rewards will come later.

3. You must be persistent. Some give up when the first obstacle comes along. Some give up when they don't make a thousand dollars within one week of starting.

Some give up before they develop the "feel" that they need for some tasks. You have to learn to sell without selling. How do you that? You have to develop a feel for that type of communication.

Why Some Marketers Quit in Frustration?

One of the biggest mistakes many affiliate marketers make is quitting the game too soon. It's very easy to see why this can happen. But the most important thing to remember is NOT to give up too soon.

To begin, it's necessary to stress the fact that affiliate marketing is not a get rich quick system. It is very rare when someone with absolutely no experience whatsoever starts generating a four and five figure income in their very first month, let alone after six months.

When it comes to building an online business that spits out cash day in and day out, week in and week out like you see on some of those ClickBank shots that some vendors use to promote their products, it's important to understand that results like that are not typical and have been achieved through... cumulative effort.

Success online has often been compared to a snowball effect. Initially when you start promoting any product, unless you use paid advertising you're not going to see a massive amount of traffic right out of the gate.

However, when you continue to work steadily day after day adding more and more links to your site, generating more and more content for your site and consistently putting in the work that so many products neglect to tell you about, your business will begin to grow and so will your results.

A major factor that contributes to the frustration that many marketers experience on their way to success is the many distractions working online presents.

It's too easy to click a link that will take you away to an interesting article or video that can easily break your momentum and eat up your time.

There's nothing more frustrating than adding up the amount of time you spend online and contrasting that with how much of it you actually spent working to produce income and make money online with affiliate marketing.

One point you need to understand is that you need to spend days on learning techniques and tactics before you can really make money. You will need to spend a lot of time reading ebooks and articles and watch youtube videos before you can start.

A lot of marketers will just give up at this point. Yet, I can tell you that you should not give up if you really want to make money online.

In fact, you have to work hard before you can see the results. You may need to work for a few months before you can really make money.

The visitors may need to visit your website a few times before they make a purchase. In order to succeed in affiliate marketing, you need to have the right mindset. There is no way you will become rich overnight. However, if you keep working, you will succeed sooner or later!

Affiliate marketing is the easiest and fastest way to make a decent living online without breaking a sweat. The business entails promoting other people's product and sharing the revenue with the owner of the product. That said, I will tell you 5 main reasons why affiliate marketing remains the easiest way to make money online.

- **You don't need to create a product**

The product has already been created. This saves you the time, effort and money you would have spent trying to create your own product. All you need is to find a good product with a good commission of 50% or more.

· **You don't need a sales page**

Creating a sales page is one of the crossroads met by newbie marketers as it is not an easy task to continuously churn out tasty sales page with good conversion. With affiliate marketing, you don't need that. The sales page has been designed by professionals for the product you are intending to promote. In fact, one of my tip to selecting a product is to find out if the merchant sales page is convincing. If it does not convince me, then it will not convince the buyer either. Simple as that.

· **You don't need an office**

The system for receiving, processing and delivering orders is already in place. You don't need to worry yourself with issues pertaining after sales services. If it's a digital product, it is a simple download.

· You don't need big money to start-up

This is the most interesting part of this business as it requires little or no capital to start making money. The aspect that may require cash investment is the area of pay per click advertising.
But if you just starting out, you can use free traffic generating sources like forum and article marketing. In fact, I stand to be correct that the free traffic methods generate long lasting traffic than the paid ones.

· You don't need be a "guru"

Some people believe you need to be a pro to make money in affiliate marketing. That is not true. I hope you believe me now that affiliate marketing is the fastest and easiest way to make a decent living online as you don't need to create a product of your own nor create a sales page thus making the setup of the business fast and easy to implement.

Chapter III

Freelance Writing

If you do not have time to set up an affiliate website and then wait until your traffic starts to pick up before you start to see some money, then freelance writing may be something that you should look into.

Not only will you begin to see immediate results, but the results could very well be what you need in order to survive financially. You may not make as much in the beginning, as you will still be learning the ropes, but once you get the hang of it, you will begin to see some serious money.

Many people have made enough money on the internet through freelancing; some are still making money on daily basis by working as freelancers. Yet, a good number of people out there do not know how to make good use of the internet technology. If you are among the people who are looking for opportunities to make money online, you should consider freelancing.

Freelancing is very common today on the internet because it's one of the easiest ways of making money online. It is a means of making money by working for employers that need your talents.

There are many types of jobs that one can do online which include data entry work, writing, web design, programming and a whole lot of others.

Many employers are looking for people to help them in one aspect of their online business or the other. Since, freelancing does not involve any long term commitment or contract, these businesses prefer hiring the services of freelancers than hiring permanent employees.

You will find a lot of freelancing jobs if you perform a Google search. Some of the reliable freelancing sites that you may join are upwork.com, freelancer.com, textbroker.com, iwriter.com and many others. You can create an account in one or two of these sites.

However, each of these sites is unique and has specific requirements that you have to meet before you will be accepted as a member. Create account only in those freelancing sites that you meet their requirements.

One thing that you should not forget to check before creating an account with any freelancing site is the banking and withdrawal methods of the site. If the withdrawal option does not favor you or it is not available in your location, you have to sign up with another site.

Choosing your area of specialization

As it has been said above, there are many jobs that one can do online in these freelancing sites. Definitely, you will not be able to do all the available jobs. So, when you are creating your account in any of the sites, you should choose only jobs that you can do.

Most freelancers provide writing services. But there are other services that you can provide such as translation work, programming, SEO services, web design, graphics, proofreading, data entry experts, blogging, logo design, marketing and others. If you cannot do any of the jobs that require special skills, you can start with data entry, proofreading jobs and others. They are easy to do.

Check through the list of the available areas of expertise in the site that you have registered with and choose the one's that you can do. Create a professional profile and excellent portfolio. Some employers take time to check the profiles and portfolios of bidders before choosing the winning bid.

You may find it difficult to win your first job. You have to be patient. Remember, you are competing with people who have many reviews, so you need to lower your rate. Create professionally looking proposals when placing your bid. You will definitely win a project.

How Can You Make Money With Freelancing?

Very easy. Simply do a search for freelance writing jobs and you will come across many great website who are willing to hire new freelancers.

Most of them will require you to write an article on a topic of your choice for them to review and decide whether you qualify as a freelance writer. If you qualify they will usually hire you within a few days or so.

A couple of the top freelance recruiters require that you pay a monthly membership fee for optimum exposure and the ability to bid on as many jobs as you like. But if that is not in your budget, then you may want to stick to the other free resources.

But don't get me wrong, there are many legitimate writing jobs listed even on the free resource sites, so be sure to check them out first before heading over to the more popular sites.

Most of these websites are updated daily as new jobs come in, so be sure to check back often and apply to as many jobs as you like.

How Much Money Can You Make?

The amount of money you can make solely depends on you. The more you write, the more you will make, but you will have to learn how to type fast. Most freelancers make anywhere between $10 to $20 an hour just by researching and writing articles.

At first you will not make this much, as you will have to spend a lot of your time researching, but once your knowledge base grows, you will be able to write from your previous notes or your memory.

Once you can do this you will be able to pump out several articles per hour. So if you want to earn big money, then you need to bid on high paying articles, and you will be on your way to internet riches.

Working as a freelance writer is one of the most popular ways to make money online. There is plenty of work for those who love to write.

Statistics show that six out of 10 businesses are spending more on content production and that the need for eBooks, case studies, articles, and newsletters is growing at an unprecedented rate. Having a solid grasp of language and being able to write in a concise manner is a must.

Many people are able to make a full time income as freelance writers. If you want to start a career in this field, you can build your brand by establishing yourself as an exceptional writer.

Create a strong portfolio that showcases your skills. Write a few guests posts on well-established sites. If you're having a difficult time finding work, then start your own blog.

Identify some of the biggest names in your niche. Interview a few of them and write a compelling article. Submit your work to a few major online publications. Contact other bloggers and let them know about your services. By offering to write quality content for these bloggers, you are helping them save time.

Look for job opportunities on forums and bid sites. There are many online communities of writers to partner with. You can ask other writers about the latest writing gigs and share industry specific tips.

Another way to make money online as a freelance writer is to write your own eBook about a topic that you are passionate about. Lots of writers are earning hundreds of dollars with their ebooks.

Some companies hire writers to create content for online newsletters or write product reviews. If you have a background in advertising, you can write slogans for different companies.

Use social media marketing to your advantage. Create detailed profile pages that describe your services. Make your promotional content attractive and concise. Always offer significant value before asking for anything.

Check out job boards and apply for relevant writing gigs. Once you have some published articles on well-established sites, you can use your published work as reference.

Make sure your portfolio features your best work. Do not send poorly written articles to potential customers. If someone asks you to write a sample article, spend a few minutes reading through the archives of the site you are writing for.

You can also write niche articles in batches and sell them to one or more clients. If you want to make a full income as a freelance writer, learn about search engine optimization and then integrate these concepts in your articles.

Being a freelancer and working online can be just fantastic. You can work in the comfort of your home and manage your time that is most suitable to you. You are not stuck with a 9 to 5 job. Listed here are some ways of making money in freelancing.

Writer

Content is king in the online world. There are Internet marketers who are looking for freelancers to write web content, articles or blog. You can even be a news writer, an editorial writer or write feature articles. Important thing is for you to be able get the relevant content and to write well.

Web Designer

With the extensive use of the Internet by most businesses, there is a demand for those with a creative flair and technical skills to design the layout of the web pages for the business. It is not just about the site looking pretty, but about being functional so that a person browsing the site will want to spend more time on the site. Within this, there are more niche designer jobs like graphic design, logo-making, animator and a few other ways of making money online.

Developer

If you have technical skills, then there are Internet marketers and business owners who look for software development in specific areas.
While ebooks are very popular products in the online world, so are software products. The Internet marketers typically outsource these kind of activities as their time is much better spent on marketing.

Copywriter

Being a copywriter is another specialized skill requiring creativity. This requires the promotion of a person, product or service through advertisements text and even videos. A good copywriter can make a significant difference in the volume of sales that is generated.

Consultants

For those professionals with specific skills, the Internet provides an avenue to market their expertise. More businesses like to outsource specialized services to people who already have the skills and experience.

Sites for Make Money through Freelance

Below is a list of freelancing sites that can be a good avenue of earning money. You might have heard of them but might have not known so much about them. Here they are and how you can use them to your advantage.

Upwork

This is the first home for outsourcing. Many outsourcers love it. On the other hand, it is a great place to make money as a freelancer.

iWriter

This is for good article writers. You get paid depending on the quality and length of articles you write. You can earn from as low as $3 to $8 for articles of various lengths.

Mechanical Turk

This is owned by Amazon, you make money doing mini-tasks, but slightly complicated.

Microworkers

This is similar to Mechanical Turk. You make money doing simple tasks.

Fiverr

On Fiverr, you make money online performing simple tasks. Any task that you can do and charge $5.

Chapter IV
Ebook Publishing

It's not surprising that many people are wondering whether or not money can really be made with e-books given the fact that the economy is so bad. There are more opportunities today to make a lot of money with any book publishing business than ever before.

There are two basic reasons for this. The first reason has to do with the fact that lots of people are searching for answers to their questions over the internet. This trend has accelerated over the past several years and shows no sign of slowing down.

The other reason has to do with the fact that you can now get started with any book publishing business with a small budget.

There are a lots of people who love purchasing e-books

What you really need is a step-by-step guide that shows you everything you need to know about getting started with self publishing. It enables you to avoid a lot of costly trial and error. In this chapter, I'm going to give you some tips about writing a ebook no matter what niche topic you choose.

Focus on content

This is of ultimate importance. You have to make sure that what you are writing is actually helpful and interesting to other people other than yourself! This is a hard thing to do at first, but after a while you will get used to it. You will develop a feel of how your audience think and react to your new material.

Don't forget style

Do not neglect style and the visual appeal of your ebook, because ebooks do get judged by their covers. Choose a fitting and interesting cover and make sure that your ebook is well formatted.

Important Things In Ebook Publishing

These are some important things to consider before you publish your ebook:

What is the purpose of the ebook?

What topics will be covered?

Who will be writing the ebook?

What format shall the ebook be published in?

How do you distribute the ebook once it is published?

1 - What is the purpose of the ebook?

First, consider what your purpose is for publishing an ebook. Is it because you are passionate about something and just want to share it with others or are you publishing the ebook for profit? Perhaps you are publishing the ebook for branding or for marketing purposes?

Your purpose has direct consequences for the remaining of the items to consider.

2 - What topics will be covered?

If you are publishing your ebook just for sharing information, you can literally include any topics that you want to discuss. However, if it's for profit, it is crucial that you are covering topics that your readers want to know, rather than what you want to share.

One guideline used by information marketers is to brainstorm for 12 main topics - which will become the titles of 12 chapters of your ebook - and 4 sub topics under each topic.

By organizing your topics this way, it will help you focus on getting the ebook written easily.

3 - How will the ebook be written?

If you're comfortable in writing, you can attempt to write one sub topic per day. That way, in less than two months, your ebook will be completed. Otherwise, an alternative way to get your book written on your behalf is by hiring ghostwriters. It can cost anywhere from fifty dollars to thousands of dollars.

You can engage a writer over the Internet through any of the popular freelance sites where writers bid for jobs in a reverse auction manner. All you need to do is to search for "freelance writer" in your favorite search engine.

4 - How do you distribute the ebook once it is published?

There are several options you should consider. You can sell the books on your own website, or you can use platforms like amazon. If you book is a hot seller, amazon does all the marketing for you. There is a learning curve on how to do this on amazon, but once you learn it, it's a breeze.

Following are some tips for writing an ebook that I've employed over the years that have allowed me to start my own little publishing empire and it can help you as well.

Ebook Publishing: Specific Things I've Done to Write books in as Little as a Few Hours

Find Time to Write: The reason why so many people procrastinate writing an ebook is that they "have to find time to write."

Write an Outline: This is the first thing I do when I sit down to write an ebook. The reason is, it keeps me focused and on top of my niche topic. It also helps me adhere to that all-important schedule of finishing within a few days.

Note: Your ebook outline will also become a critical part of your sales page. So it serves a double purpose and is a critical part of the ebook publishing.

Don't Edit, Write: One of the reasons you can write an ebook so quickly is when you sit down to write, just write. Don't worry about editing it or polishing it, or trying to make it perfect. Just get the thoughts out of your head down on paper. Be sure to refer back to your ebook outline so you don't miss any important points.

I'm willing to bet dollars to doughnuts that if you do this, you'll have more than enough material for a 30, 40 or 50 pager if you write like this. You may even find yourself having to cut material.

Niche It: In my opinion, these little babies should be in the 30-60 page range. The reason is - again, in my experience and opinion when most people purchase an ebook, they're looking for specific information on a specific topic.
And I'm talking about "non-fiction, how to" ebooks (the kind I specialize in).

Leave Out the Fluff: Notice the title of this book. It's very specific. When you read this, it had darned well better give you info about this - not about publishing in general, what size font to use, how to format page, etc.

You probably clicked on this book because you wanted info on how to make money online, right?

Edit/Revise/Rewrite: Once you have the info down, then you can spend a day or so rewriting and organizing your material. But please don't spend too much time on this. You can edit or revise to death and it'll never be "quite right" (or make you money). But, you'll never know unless you publish it.

The Best Way to Market to Get Quick Sales

Now that the writing is done, it's time to market. I use article marketing and posting ads on free classified ad sites like backpage. Usually, when I first publish an ebook, I'll write 20-30 articles during the first month (using SEO strategies to get search engine juice).

Then, I may keep that up and write one article a week for the next 4-5 months. Over time, this may drop off to 2-3 articles a month, forever. I also market to my in-house list of newsletter subscribers and via my social media (Twitter) account.

If you follow these steps, you can literally publish one ebook per week and you can be on your way to creating your own ebook publishing empire.

Ebook Marketing

Marketing a book is a multi-task project that requires several different types of solutions. Many authors consider ebooks a new, and different marketing channel for their books. You can increase your sales and free time by creating your own marketing timeline.

The important part of the ebook phenomenon is that any ebook can be converted easily into an audio eBook, one of the fastest growing segments on the internet today. In fact we have a product that can automate the conversion process for you.

In addition to ebook publishing being the fastest way to get published today, it's an exciting new way to make extra income from the internet.

As opposed to written text in a physical form such as books and magazines, ebooks are items which can be published in a quick manner. As soon as the writer is finished writing the ebook, they can be well on their way to having it published online.

The way in which the internet works allows individuals to take their ideas, whether it be in the form of ebook publishing or otherwise, and then put it online as soon as they are ready to do so. This quick way of publishing this variety

of written material makes producing
ebooks quiet easy.

One if the reasons why ebook publishing
is the fastest way to make money online is
that this type of web content can be
distributed to a large group of individuals
all at once.
Those who may be considering ebook
publishing as a way to gain a quick
income online will also find that they will
be able to keep much of the money that is
paid to them by purchasers due to the fact
that there is little or no overhead involved.

All that writing and publishing is really is
a one time thing. Since the book will be
delivered in a digital format, there is no
overhead involved.

And if your ebook is listed on amazon, the
owner of the book can simply sit back and
relax while their ebook basically sells
itself.

As opposed to a web content writer who
has to constantly submit new articles to be

paid, ebook writers need only write the book once and then have it be sold over and over again. It will never expire and unlike retail products, you never need to aquire new inventory. You set up your book once and collect passive income for life.

This is another important reason why ebook publishing is the fastest way to make money online and something which all web content producers should considering doing.

Chapter V
Domain Flipping

If you are a home-based person who want to make money the fastest way possible, here are some online websites that could help you.

For some who want to earn money with less effort, there is what we call Domain Flipping.

For those not familiar with the term, flipping websites derives its name from real estate flipping, where you buy a distressed property, add value by fixing it up, and then turning around and selling, or flipping, it for a quick profit.

With website flipping, often you create a website from scratch to sell quickly, although you can be successful in this business by buying a previously owned website, fixing it up, and then flipping for fast cash.

Either way, you add value to the site by generating traffic and revenue. At this point, you can either hang onto this "virtual real estate" and realize even greater long term profit, or flip it for a quick pay day.

The process of learning how to flip websites is not that difficult. There are no complicated formulas or confusing scripts to set up.

Anyone with a computer and online access can get started in this business. In addition, there are no large upfront fees required to get started; basically just a domain name and hosting, which can be had for less than $20.

Today the most common platform used for website creation is a WordPress blog. The script that is required to set up a WordPress blog is free, and can even be set up with just a few clicks with basic hosting.

There are hundreds of free Themes or Templates you can use to give your website/blog its appearance.

The versatility of the WordPress platform doesn't stop with all the themes available. You can also add what are called "plugins." As with themes, there are thousands of plugins available online that can further enhance the value of a given website. Some plugins require a fee, but the vast majority of them can be used for free.

If you've had enough of bouncing from one Internet project to another and are finally serious about making money online, it's time you learned how to flip websites.

Flipping websites requires very little money or expertise, so virtually anyone with a desire to succeed can make money with this business model.

Flipping a domain name entails buying one domain which would generate a lot of traffic because of popularity, and selling it for a specific amount. You just need to have quick and smart thinking in entering domain flipping business.

Many people have been successful in this business mainly because it is very much like buying and selling. Domain names are the specific names of websites found in their URL. In buying a domain, you must make sure that the name is commonly searched by browsers.

Popular search keywords from search engines are what business man all over the world are looking for in domains because it would generate considerable visits. You can now browse domain names that are popular in search engines in GodDaddy.com and in sedo.com, and buy them for about $10-$15.

You should find a domain that would be easy to maintain and monetize. Monetizing means adding advertisements that could encourage more visitors.

As a starter, you could sell the domain name for a good profit in Sedo or eBay. The longer you maintain a certain domain, the higher you could price it. This is a fast make money online path.

How does this business work?

There are two different known techniques to do website flipping: build a web site and sell it for a profit or buy a web site for a cheap price (or discount price), make some modifications and improvements to it and resell it for a higher price.

There are several marketplaces that you can use to sell websites and domains online; for example: sedo.com, flippa.com and many different webmaster forums like digitalpoint.com.

One of the important advantage of this sort of business is you have a chance to make a lot of money if you know how to do it the right way.

In order to achieve success with this business you should either possess some skills including web design and development, graphic design, content writing and some basic search engine optimization and internet marketing knowledge; or have enough money to hire someone to do the job for you.

There are numerous available ebooks on the internet that explain all the particulars and details of this business including purchasing or making a website, how to make the site profitable and how to sell it online.

Ways to Maximize Your Domain Flipping Profits

Many people refer to domains as virtual real estate. Because of that, domain flipping is quickly becoming as popular and profitable as house flipping. The only problem with domains is that online, people think that they can do everything quicker.

Virtual real estate takes time just like physical real estate does. Follow these tips to maximize your profits in domain and site flipping.

1. Patience is key in practically anything and everything you do in life. Things can't be rushed - especially important things. If you want to flip a domain to make the most money possible, you need to be patient and allow the domain to age.

People don't like to buy domains that are new on the web. Newly registered domains don't have any traces in search engines which is the main reason buyers avoid registering their own domains. They want to buy from someone who's already given the domain a little reputation.

2. Don't leave the website sitting. Even if you don't feel like making content or putting up a website script, the worst thing you could do is allow your domain registrar to rake in all the profits from the domain parking. At least park your

domain under your own account to get the few dollars that it generates.

3. Another way to maximize your profits in domain flipping is to put up a website script or content page. Adding website content to your domain not only gets it indexed in search engines, but it also sends a little traffic. You could even charge extra to include the website with the domain when it's time to sell.

4. For those who want to make a profit worth a year's salary, it really doesn't even take much more work. It takes smarter work. To increase your gains even more, build a content site with multiple pages.

Do just a small bit of promoting, build some backlinks, and get a good amount of traffic flowing. If you can do this for about three or four months, you could see a profit of 300 percent.

Maximizing your profit in domain flipping isn't challenging at all. It simply takes time which most investors are scared to spend. However, if one were to do so, he or she would see profits ten times what they are seeing now. Many people make a living doing this.

Chapter VI
Google Adsense

There are plenty of online methods available for you to make money fast. Before you enroll in such program consider the various pros and cons associated with it. You also need to ensure that the fast online money making program that you are enrolling is not fraud.

Today, online market has opened new possibilities for making money online fast. This concept of earning money is gaining popularity, especially when there is acute joblessness in the market due to global liquidity crunch.

Just imagine you are making easy money every week in the comfort of your own home.

What can be a better option of earning easy money than this? Your passion to write or shoot photos can be an easy method to earn money. And there is Google AdSense for you, the most trusted and convenient online marketing tool available today.

You will of course try to increase your income from this system. So try the simple and unique Google Home Business Kit program which is a Three Stars Google Profit System.

With the help of this program making passive income every day is almost guaranteed. You can definitely earn as much as you can from the Google Home Business Kit, but at the same time you have to keep on increasing the number of websites from few to many as possible.

You can try out any of the following convenient methods to making money online fast:

Putting up videos:

You can't even imagine that your videos can fetch you easy money. What you can do is create a short documentary like video on some interesting topic and publish it on your blog or website. Now when your site or blog starts attracting visitors, promptly link this system's Ads with it.

Whenever, a visitor visits your site/blog and clicks on the ads you earn money. To increase the readership of your site/blog you can post recent updates about your site on various social networking sites such as Orkut and Facebook. So, more visitors click on the ads you get more money online.

Writing for earning:

If you have a passion for writing than make money doing what you love. Wondering how is it possible? There are many free blog sites available such as WordPress or Blogspot where you can register for free and start blogging.

You can write on any topic that you feel comfortable with. When your blog gets popular then include Google's advertising program Ads in it. By doing this you can earn money while satisfying your passion to write.

Doing so you do not have to worry about your 9-5 job anymore or your financial situation because you have built your own passive income that earns you money even when you are sleeping, while you are on vacation, or when you are spending time with your family on the beach or anywhere else in the world.

Just about anybody who pursues internet marketing does so with the express wish to make extra money online fast. The problem is that 'fast' is a very debatable word. Many people consider 'fast' to be overnight while other consider 'fast' to be within a few weeks or a month or two in the future.

However, when you consider making money online you should consider which ventures will actually continue to produce extra money not only now but also in the future.

Google AdSense is a unique program created for individuals who run websites and blogs. With this program you simply place advertisements on your website and you receive money in relation to how many people visit your pages where these advertisements are placed and additionally you make extra money each time a person clicks on one of these advertisements.

If your website or blogs receive a substantial amount of 'hits' each month you could be making hundreds or thousands of dollars each month.

It is definitely possible to make extra money online fast with Google AdSense. All you have to do is place these advertisements on your website and drive traffic to your website. The more traffic that your website receives, the more money that you will make.

Put a little effort behind your website planning and assure that you strategically place your advertisements where they will be noticed the most and you can rest assured Google AdSense will do all the rest.

If you want to be like most people online than you will want to reach that goal of $100 a day, but how do you make $100 a day with Google AdSense? The trick to making money with AdSense is to understand the numbers.

What I mean by this is that on average no matter what topic you are covering the numbers show that between 1 and 3 people out of 100 will click on the Google ads.

And depending on what topic you are covering and which keywords your website is themed to will give you your daily total.

For example if you wanted to create a website on "Making money online" then your average click would make you around $1.50, so all you would have to get per day is 67 clicks. And in order for you to figure out which words to target you can check that out using Google's keyword tool.

Now that you understand the numbers I want to give you a few tips on how to make $100 a day with Google AdSense. The first thing you need to do is come up with 10 different topics that you would like to write about.

If you can't come up with 10 then try 5, the reason I want you to get more than one is because it is easier to have multiple websites earn less than having one website earn all the money and get all the traffic.

If you can come up with 10 different topics then you can make 10 different websites and that would mean you only need to make $10 from each website.

What I normally do is create one website and get it to make $5 per day and then move on to my next website; that way I am not over working and not taking care of my other sites. Just think if you had 20 sites all making between $5 and $10 per day.

And the last tip I have for you is that if you are serious about Google AdSense to make cash fast then you won't give up and you will keep writing articles and building backlinks to get your site where you want it. Making money with Google AdSense can be tough, but if you just look at the numbers and pick topics you love then it will all work out very well for you.

Chapter VII

How to Achieve Success with Making Money Online

Possessing great confidence while chasing after your dreams and goals is a great thing to have. However, being confident is usually not quite enough to give you the edge you need to become successful. Achieving success on the internet is no different.

Besides having a positive attitude, it is vital that you know and accept the harsh realities of internet marketing as well. This is an important, yet often overlooked step that separates success and failure online.

Facing the hard truths of Internet marketing is not about thinking negatively. It's accepting and understanding that there will be many obstacles and even disappointments on your path to success on the internet.

When you know what obstacles you can encounter, you dramatically decrease your chances of failure because you are well prepared.
Over 95% of people who start a marketing business online fail at making money.

A majority of these people did not prepare for the obstacles that every successful internet marketer eventually encounter. They probably possessed plenty of confidence and maybe a lot of enthusiasm and passion as well.

However, they created a stage for failure because they simply ignored the realities of making money online. It's not always the individual's ego or carelessness that gets them in trouble. Internet marketing hype is a big factor that sets many up for disappointment.

How often have you run into promises of fast, easy money online? It never will work that way, and there are countless people who give up easily after they discover that harsh reality.

The correct attitude will start your momentum to becoming financially independent online. But, you can fall fast and hard at any given time if you didn't accept the harsh realities of Internet marketing.

So, you must realize that you may not make any money online for months that it could take a fairly good amount of effort and time on your part, or you may have to invest more money than you want.

Realities like these should always be kept in mind. If they do happen, you are in a much better situation to overcome them and to continue on.

Accepting and knowing the possible hardships you may encounter while on the journey to success is all about being well prepared. Besides, you would not show up for an important test at school unless you were prepared.

You're probably going to fail it even with the best attitude in the world. Preparing for what obstacles can pop up during your journey to financial wealth online is an extremely important step that too many people skip or ignore. Don't allow yourself to jump in the crazy world of internet marketing without good, solid preparation.

A great attitude and being well prepared, especially for certain hardships, is a winning and lucrative combination in the world of online marketing.

It's a definite advantage that will leap you over your competitors and place you in the minority of entrepreneurs who are actually making a great living online. It can be accomplished and there's no reason why you can't do it.

While some Internet Marketers may claim that money can easily be made online, it requires more than simply the belief that you can do it. The technical barriers have come down, and today it is possible for non-technical people to readily access this business space.

However, as in the off-line world, appropriate attention to all three of the following drivers will greatly increase your success:

1. Passion - Identifying and focusing on what you are interested in is the key place to start. If you focus on your passion, you will unlock your enthusiasm and energy and you will be more likely to put in the effort required to succeed.

2. Knowledge - Gathering the necessary knowledge and information about how to be successful and make money online is the next critical element.

It makes good sense to gather sufficient knowledge and understanding from experts to avoid foreseeable mistakes in online business. The internet is stocked full of sources of this information, but watch out that you do not waste time gathering more and more information as a block to making money.

3. Action - Taking action now and not procrastinating is what will separate you into the group of people that achieve success. Take action to identify your passion and gather knowledge as your first two steps.

Keep the momentum up and implement your new found knowledge as soon as you can. Having the passion and knowledge, without taking action to implement it will not deliver the results you seek. Taking action now is the key to success.

Conclusion

It takes time to learn the score and get to grips with the various methods available, especially if you want to achieve success with very little outlay. There is no secret way to get rich quick online. When you work from home people, such as family and friends think you are not working at all, so people will think you're free to meet them for coffee, lunch, or dinner.

I soon came to realize I had to get tough and to say no. You will have to do the same. It is important to draw up a schedule that you can stick to. Set aside a definite time to devote to building up your business.

Decide today what you want out of life. Is it the fabulous lifestyle, the exotic holidays or the big house? Perhaps you just want a better standard of living for your family. Whatever it is, come to understand the power of a single decision acted upon immediately and with utter conviction.

All of us possess inner resources, something to which we can turn for help, that can enable us to achieve all we have ever dreamed of. A single decision can open the floodgates to joy or sorrow, prosperity or want, companionship or loneliness, long life or early death.

Could you make a decision today that could change or improve your quality of life? Just remember, all decisions have consequences. Failing to make a decision is a decision in itself. Think of two actions you need to do right now that will change your life.

Decide now - this is it! Remember - Stay Focused to make money online.

"Live the Life You've Dreamedof"

www.ingramcontent.com/pod-product-compliance
Lightning Source LLC
Chambersburg PA
CBHW070504220526
45467CB00002B/559